# A Mirror More ...ul

# A Mirror More Truthful

Tuhin Sanyal

*Chitrangi*

*A Mirror More Truthful*
Published by Chitrangi Foundation

A-10/1, Amarabati, Sodepur,
Kolkata 700110, INDIA

Contact: chitrangifoundation@gmail.com

Copyright: Tuhin Sanyal
First edition (Paperback): December, 2017
Printed and bound at S. P. Communications, Calcutta.



Cover photograph, concept and design:
Bitan Chakraborty

ISBN-13: 978-81-934230-0-4

Price: INR 250 | USD 8.99

To life and other trivia

# Acknowledgements

Ma, Raina*ma*,
Life force
&
*Chitrangi Foundation*

# Contents

Love

Dark, dead-ends
love
the taste of light;
there, walls grope
for refuge.
And sighs mistake
sour kernels
for the sweetness
of a drooping tree.

Gabriel

Gabriel,
I'm crushing mature grapes
and dark-chocolates in my mouth;
I'm enjoying the thick ooze
flood my willing throat!
Teardrop-crystal chandeliers
are chiming in
as Spirit-ditties to my mind!
The breeze
is flirting with speed,
and time is crystallizing
like some careful cyanide
in my heart!

Gabriel,
I'm re-reading *Love
in the Time of Cholera*
in a speedy train!

Plastic Stars

The book of reckoning
Opens after sunset,
Fingers calculate
The orbit of a lie,
The heart settles
For an age-old tendency,
And plastic stars
Spell 'anarchy'
From the sky!

A Mirror More Truthful

A form
and formal attire
could be the way of life,
a tattered coat
might be casual wear,
and a broken tie,
a necessity!
But when all coalesce
to form a shadow,
they search
for a mirror more truthful
and void
of mercuric sham!

Monsoon

With loans and promises disbursed
after petty signatures,
an afternoon became important
in equal installments,
as a cackling baby girl
waved from the glass-window
through the rain!

The market flushed its ire
through the Sunday commode,
a minimalist woman tripped
and a bohemian man pulled over,
as a cackling baby girl
threw lozenges at them
through the rain!

The sun tried prying into a CCD
but the misty A.C.s flung it out,
unhappy couples held routine hands
as the beggar clasped his head,
and a cackling baby girl
showed them taffeta dolls
through the rain!

The market and men turned
to the glass-window
o'er the haggard shack;
through lozenges, taffeta, dolls,
came waving her beckoning calls,
and that nebulous baby girl
shed her love in tears
and spat at adult years
through the rain!

Can You Fly?

Diamonds grow in the sky.
Trust me,
I've read the cosmos!
But, can you fly?

Of Calculations

Earthly co-ordinates are slaves
To latitudes and longitudes,
And easy equations
Are tethered to the earth.
The earthly co-ordinates
Do not realize
There is a whole universe
Of incalculable birth
Above their heads;
Untrodden, unkempt!

Free Play

beyond a nightmare
eglantines
can be rewritten

across the rivers
knee deep scars
laze in the mitten

springs pass the new eyes
of an old fish
tears kill the goldfish

Confusions

Beauteous can be body,
Or, beauty can be brain,
Bathe in my baritone,
Oh darling, once again!

Cadences can be pleasure,
But music can be pain,
Singly pipe your body-flute
(As) minor, major, plain!

Your body is now thoughtful
And skeptic, once again,
Think between your thighs, Love,
And tell me where to rain!

A Portrait of this Sky

Between this evening and sickness
Keep some *Doctor Scholl*,
When red hutments quake and quiver
Holding the skies
In abdominal fall.

I too am below the same sky—
Walking
The avian fires of death-muck;
Since every road is a diary-entry,
I write before I walk.

Younger sisters, or the one
Between siblings,
Are short notes or bonsai
Or shrubbery saplings;
Soft!

With a sun aloft,
And yet, below the sky
Since my birth,
Rain-covetous flowers
Question the dumb desires
Of the wanton earth—

This body.

This sky is a lopsided nobody—
A gesture of birds,
And their nervous disorders,
Or perhaps their spleen,
Or even nectarine,
Or perhaps their prison, flame,
Or water,
Expanse unlimited (all the same),
Lie severed!

Severed from the waves and flux,
Cut off from the high,
Well severed from everything
That wants to be this sky!

A Promise

Fine years have passed,
And fine long winters
Have graced their heels
Where summer saunters!

Do wait for me
Where warmth may be,
Where fruition all
Is tapestry!

There love galore
Is kept in store
For the innocent kid
And wanton whore!

The Scribe

Stories of ash-pits
And darkness combine,
A separate Gibraltar
Lives the myth,
Babel stoops
To hear their tale,
I write it all
On a monolith.

A Cremation on Christmas Day

Today wasn't the first.
Many-a-time to that burning-*ghat* have I been—
Be it Eid, Diwali, Christmas or Halloween—
To burn someone known or close to me.

Today wasn't the first
That soulless bodies lay in a humble queue,
For the non-experience of something new—
To burn in body, yet, not feel the heat.

I sat before the Ganga,
An open sky to behold,
When someone burnt away
With body's liquid gold.

The sunny incinerator
Took in the bodies, cold!
And slammed doors on follies
Of humans, young and old.

A mist of silky smoke
From those burnt and dead—
Arose, like my thought,
Which the Ganga reflected.

Death perfects Art—
"To be or, not to be"—
Life's literature scores
More than Comedy.

Raina's Earth

Thrice, my toddler's feet and mine,
Wove charms around that food-court fine,
Took rounds of three when we both ran,
She—'Robin,' I—'Spiderman,'
Older gazes gauged our ground,
My toddler yelled, "The earth is round!"
And every circle which we made
In wilting sun and raining glade,
Turned evening into chocolate-drops,
And ice-creams and jolly-pops,
And apple-juice and *firni*-bowls
And kisses for two magic-souls!
Since earth is flat and so are feet,
We did our best to make them meet,
With bolder gaze on older ground
My Raina yelled, "The earth is round!"

# Your Island is my River

Your island is my river,
Your fixity, my flux!
My eye-consciousness
Your dream inducts!

Your stones turn liquid
As light. (Flood my room!)
False gods drown there
To pave that petty doom!

Cinchona nights are bitter,
Like fragrant, empty beds;
Fixity in flux, rather
Than heartless, empty heads!

Senses

Avoiding every bad bend,
Five make it to the end!
Sight, Smell, Taste, Touch & Sound
Fortify their ground.
Grounds are but graveyards
Where Senses coagulate,
Every Birth is a weakling
At the hands of Fate!

Robots

They toiled to learn…
                    All the books by rote,
Resolved to pull…
                    Shutters 'pon their hearts,
Rationale…
                    With information smote,
Mustered all…
                    To be sold in business-marts.

Four Quartets

Summer took my vest,
And Winter took my coat,
Spring took my flower-vase,
Monsoon, my paper-boat!

The Fleeting Mermaid

On my lips
Her love is a dusky din,
Ah! Riverine love...
She flaunts a dorsal fin,
O Mermaid meet,
I love your silver cleft,
Lip-service—
I kiss but a fleeting chin!

Vibgyor

Dearth of colors…
And a few broken crayons
Caught my fancy.
Violet, Indigo,
Blue, Green,
Yellow, Orange and Red,
But they all
Colored it
Grey inside my head!

Day-end and double-malt
Were colors too,
But they merely
Darkened the hue.

And I sat up
Through the long night,
As if in power-cut,
Memory-bites and pain;
I started rummaging
Through darkness again
In my plight,
Till I found a match-stick
To my sheer delight.

I lit it up
To my soul,
And saw VIBGYOR
In a flash of light.

The Dancing Girl of Mohenjo-Daro

There were rail-tracks in Mohenjo-Daro,
And there were bullet-trains,
Discos, and night-pubs too,
And all the urban banes!

Love ran through rail-tracks there,
Hatred, through drainage, planned;
Democracy was in every heart,
Dictatorship was banned.

Yes, I fell in love there,
With the Dancing Girl, now wry.
Her bronze figurine stands today
In the museum I pass by!

She stepped out thence and history books
To hit the cover of 'Time,'
She dances now to different tunes
And hates the lover of rhyme.

Connoisseurs do test her age,
They touch the artifact,
Curators now polish her,
(For) she, in polish, lacked!

Maverick, three thousand years!
She sees herself as young.
Maverick, three thousand years!
I too loved her that long.

Sundry lovers pump her heart
To make good of her lie,
In myriad loves she lost her art;
None can indemnify!

She locks her soul in caskets false
And lies all through her way,
But cleans the mess when evening falls,
Cries at the end of day.

When museum hours are over,
I call up her old landline,
She sobs and says, "Don't torture me,
I'm bathing in my brine!"

Time-Travel

A kiss on a silky neck,
A warm hug, a decent peck,
Historic girl and modern man,
A different love, a flouted ban!

Dew

If you have two good palms,
Pray, do not pray for alms,
Catch the world in a drop of dew!
If you have good eye-sight,
Pray, bask in your own light,
Let diamond-droplets smile at you!

Before Pieta

In the beginning
they plotted his death,
then they celebrated his birth,
and said "Merry Christmas!"
to each other.

Then, someone created a 'Pieta!'

Die on a Sunday

A Sabbath dawn do choose.
'Tis best to die on a Sunday,
If we have to die one day,
Let it be a happy morn
After the weekend-booze!

A death is no great matter,
We'll die past coffee-cup-clatter,
When grandchildren pour milk on flakes of corn.
Our 'day-off' sons or daughters
Shall get time for the ritual waters,
And sprinkle it from a plastic jug
On our jovial Sunday morn.
Ah! Holiday-happy dawn!

Advocates of our 'wills,'
Executors of our 'deeds,'
On a video-calling Sabbath day
Shall name our "chosen seed(s)."

For those irregular nurses,
And the drivers of the hearses,
'Tis a snoring Sunday, fun-day for them too!
With drills of checking purses,

With sighs and stifled curses,
They'll forget Death shall someday love them
too!

'Tis best—a Sunday ride;
By which, in life, we abide!
Why not a final 'hearse-ride afternoon?'
With post-lunch desserts tried,
None shall ask, "Who died?"—
Death on Sunday is a perfect boon!

A Father's Forte

When the best part of your soul,
Say, your little daughter,
Waits for you at a distance,
I bet you'll wade through the water!

May be you know not swimming,
Even so, you cannot fly,
Yet you'll grow your fins and wings
To give it a perfect try!

Maxim

It really hurts
when you find
the last peanut
in your earthen bowl
blanched!
But since it's the last of the lot,
and your own,
you still want to nibble on parts
you can salvage!

If a Spark…

If a sundry spark
Kisses your white shirt
Black near the chest,
Remember to wear it
Only in winter
Under a pullover.

That way,
Your collars shall be seen,
Spotless and white.

A Beaver's Birthday

When life-force is fever,
Its potion fits the spoon;
The living one—a beaver—
Jumps up to touch the moon!

Sweet honey, sepia…
The busty beaver sips,
And weia-lalla-leia—
He licks the flower-tips.

Butterflies a-flutter!
The beaver spins a web,
Ushers in some warmth
On the coldest *Sixth of Feb*!

Sepia

I had money enough in my wallet
To buy a rose and a river-bed,
I squandered all for novelty,
And brought home a lie instead.

I bartered some rainbow thoughts,
Got sepia feelings in exchange,
Sepia pictures skirted off
Other hues from sepia range!

Sepia hue, I mistook you
When truth was just an answer-sheet,
Good-night, Love, but tomorrow
You'll find some worms in your pleat!

Mermaids in Your Soup

You must have sea-fish in your soup,
Or mermaids, once in a while,
Prised open at the waist
To be had in perfect style!

You must have bumpkins (platter rate!)
That Tony Lumpkin's way,
No rumbling of your grumbling ale
Shall scoff at you this day!

Try, be true to falsity,
As false cities do bare
Treasures through their low-waist jeans
And topless nightmare!

Hold 'em all, the rise and fall,
The minor, major, sharp;
Aeolian damsels sway
To oomph oozing harp!

Pixie-pat! Turn diplomat
When heavens go astray,
Things hell-bound shall all come round,
We'll meet on a better day!

Last Light in the Backyard

Last light in the backyard,
Roots dug up by mice,
Feline form—the setting sun
Dips itself in ice!

Supper is a fallen thing,
Power-cuts are fine,
Photographs are memories
Mine, only mine!

Night comes to sup again,
Sits beside my seat,
Shadows become flickered light
Beneath my fickle feet!

Music meets dream's corridor,
Invalidates the sun,
And night postpones love
Just for fun!

Valentine's Day is Like Playing Chinese Whisper

Valentine's Day is like
Playing Chinese Whisper,
*Love* moves from (y)ear to (y)ear
To keep the game on;
By the time 'tis given out
The initial *love* is gone!

*Umrao Jaan* as *Don Juan*,
*V-Day* as *D-Day* stands,
*Manicured* is *Teddy-cured*
(Refrain from holding hands!)

*Kisses* become *chocolate-sauce*,
*Jam* turns into *sham*,
*Veggie lass* is *Lady Loss*
And *hammers* become *ham*!

Say *old wife*, hear *civil strife*,
Say *brawny lass*, hear *crass*,
*Beethoven* turns *well-shaven*,
*Godzilla*, *Gunter Grass*!

Loves travel from (y)ear to (y)ear,
My loves are twenty-ten,

If Love is like that Chinese Whisper,
Must I love again?

Neo-Genesis

In the beginning…
There was Darkness and Chaos,
Then light flooded
Through shopping malls.

Dwindling fell Love's water,
God left his dilapidated quarter,
To snore away in empty stalls.

When he settled for a gnome,
Mortals offered him
A new home,
But 'twas all the same,
He preferred the A.T.M.!

Vision

There may be moments
When I
Am just beside you
And yet you cannot see me;

Moments when I drive you down
The alleys,
Curves and bends,
Through the musical evenings
Towards the book-store;
There may be moments galore
That parchment lends,
Beyond the church-bells
Where Prufrock talks of oyster-shells,
And I
Whisper sweet nothings
Into your ear;

Moments of trembling kisses,
A soft hand wiping a tear;

And when you cannot see me
At such moments dear,
I too feel blind.

There may be moments
Of forgotten roads
And remembered lanes,
Moments of sober days
And hurricanes,
Moments of utter darkness
And blinding light,
Moments of blindness
And failing sight;

If you cannot see me then,
Though love lingers,
Simply close your eyes
To see me with your fingers!

Masks

One cannot deny
masquerade strategies,
nor whine.
Masks make us even
at odds,
and sometimes unruly,
like wine.

Fire

When some fire looks at you
From the upper-berth
In a train,
Make sure the blanket
You tuck yourself in
Is thick!

Make sure no corner
Is slack,
Make sure
No darkness is visible
When you look back!

Oh! But patiently bear,
My experience tells—
The fire that teases you
Shall soon look away
And gut someone else!

The Story of a Poet

He made a tree
And hid it
In the overgrowth.
Its trunk (and barks),
Thicket-smitten,
Well hidden
From human view,
Called for a sky.
Its roots
Went in deep
And sang a lullaby
To every grave!

Ghouls arose from sleep.
Maggots forgot brunch.
Skulls fed on shoulder-bones
But He skipped His lunch!

Then He made a breeze,
Scattered...
Among the woods;
Its flux got
Ticket-smitten,
Went unwritten

In all the books.
The breeze
Called for a sky.
Its sigh
Went in deep
And sang a lullaby
To every single grave!

Harlot-bodies woke
Every pimp with punch.
Love fed on smolder-cones
But He skipped His lunch.

Then He made His verse,
Buried below the tree;
The poet's strife
In Eden forms
A unique canopy!

## Old Primary and Antithetical New

I keenly observe changes
in the natural order,
on the face of my city,
in my daughter,
and in those who are close to me.

What I do not understand
comes and stands
straight before my eyes
to make its point, with emphasis.

I re-think, and I re-view!

I find an untrodden universe,
a new cosmos perhaps
that has to pay a price
when it stands erect
in front of the old order.

Not all erections are welcome,
neither the payment easy,
but the earth will remain spherical
even in my unholy dream.

Coffee-Love, besides Teaching

My 7.30 mornings are epic!
Fresh faces, mingled with dew,
Unlearn to learn about
Literary wonders new!

Freud stands beside them
With theories on the white-board,
Lacan wakes from slumber
And hits the road!

Yeats churns his poems again,
Joyce sums up all,
Impressions and expressions
Run up to Nature's call!

Modernism lights the stove,
Structuralist wipes the spoon,
My ideological 'coffee-love'
Sugars me till noon!

To Press My Cheek

Tonight, in the afternoon,
I touched a waxing moon
With my cheek!
I canoed up the rainbow
After waiting
For an extra week.

The moon was farther up,
Facing the Urals
(Or perhaps the Alps)
With a smile,
(So) I rowed an extra mile!

Ah! Farther I rowed,
Dear daughter;
I rowed on colors seven!
To press my cheek
Upon the Eye of Heaven!

A Promise from a Father to his Daughter

Raina,
Very soon I shall tell you
The story of this earth!
I shall tell you why
Mountains grow tall,
Why the spring
Precedes the fall,
Why the azure, nightly sky
Waits for the birth
Of morn, and why
The fire creates a ring
At Tierra-del-Fuego!

Well, darling,
Together shall we go
To the sea
Where the sun shines;
There we shall be,
And I shall tell you why
The living conch whines
When you hold it up
To your ear,
Why the red-crabs
Scurry away in fear,

Why the foams falter
On the shores
That it cannot alter!

And I shall talk of oars,
And the small fishing boats
Where heroic souls vie
And fish;
I shall tell you, aye,
Of leaning men
In tattered coats
And a holy wish!

I shall tell you how
The banyans grow,
And how the canyon-rills,
Which go down to the sea,
Came from the hills!

I shall talk of mountains,
Show you the deodar and pine,
Poplars, willows and canes,
And how strawberries entwine!

I shall tell you all,
I'll tell you all in due time;

But I shall talk of human beings
After your nursery rhyme!

Rewriting those Irish Gravestones

"The grave is a fine and private place."

— Andrew Marvell
(*To His Coy Mistress*)


*Remember me! O' passer-by,*
*As you are now so once was I!*
*As I am now so you shall be;*
*Prepare yourself to follow me!*

*Yes, traveler! Here, cast an eye,*
*As you are now so once was I!*
*Prepare in time, make no delay...*
*For youth and time will pass away.*

*Once I stood where thou dost now;*
*And viewed the dead as thou dost me,*
*Ere long thou'lt lie like me;*
*Others shall stand and look on thee!*

Yet, trust me, I won't be content
Until I know which way you went!
Be my shadow, be my ghoul,
But never be a skimpy soul!

Call me up when you are dead,

Call me up in colors red,
I shan't talk back to you love,
I shall clean your tainted bed!

Roses, Daisies, there shall bloom,
'Love-making' shall seek no room,
"The grave is a fine and private place"
Where all your loves you may embrace!

On Time

Passing Time is statistics
In frequencies and class,
It traces metalanguage,
Reflects on broken glass!

Gyres create patterns new—
Triad, Cone and Square,
Time breaks untimely
And scatters everywhere.

O figment of fragmented time--
Time Fractus—true,
Wake up in my daughter's rhyme
With your nascent hue!

Petrushka

I thought it was a bastard
shouting at me;
on closer scrutiny
I found it
to be a puppet,
under the effect of ventriloquism!

Pity,
even the words
were not his own!

"What's in a Name?"

He asked: "What's a taboo?"
I said: A beef-eating Hindu!
(He didn't understand.)

She asked: "What's a taboo?"
I said: A pork-eating Muslim!
(She didn't understand.)

A Third asked: "Sir, what's a taboo?"
This time I answered,
"Sex, Condom, Sunny Leone and…"
And then,
I took my name!

Trust me, they all understood!

To Eve

I wish I could sell my dreams
To earn some brownie-points,
I wish I could ply in love
With history in my joints.
I wish I could stop your watch
And stall your straying heart,
I wish I could try your lies
At your business-mart.
I wish you were apple-tree
And I, the apple fine,
Sweet, in her sourness,
Eve's a nectarine!
I wish you were taxis'-strike,
For boatmen would then ply,
I wish you were never you,
Forever you were I!
But wishes, if, were horses, love,
Beggars too would ride,
This is mere poem, love,
No inkling of a snide!

Tonight

If I am allowed
To be a cloud
And flout the social norms,
I shall tell someone why...
I paint her softness
On the nightly sky.

I shall tell her tonight
Why I miss her,
And I'll pick up a fight
In a bid to kiss her
If she turns me down.

I'll tell her to wear
That pink gown—
Strawberry-pink, in the milky-way;
I'll tell her to sway
In my cosmos
Night and day.

Tonight, I'll tell her
To burn and blaze,
And well erase
Memories

From our previous birth;
Tonight—
We'll bask in mirth.

Or, I may recite
'Marvel' tonight
Over the phone,
Or 'Eliot'—
That 'Love Song…'
Of feeling alone.

Or, must I just
Sit tight?
Or…
Call her up
And say, "Good night?"

Will she hang up,
Or lay bare
Her emotions
And say, "I care?"

Her 'careful thoughts'—
I trespass them;
And start dreaming
At 10 p.m.!

Snail Mail

Happy were those early days
When we would write
Letters
Stating *Yours Truly*
On paper.

The snail-mails
Would carry our emotions,
Slowly,
To those who cared.

On the other distant end,
They would silently wait—
Fifteen days,
Or a month or two or three—
In parlors, arm-chairs, fields
Or fresco-caves;
They waited for an emotion
To arrive!
And they waited happily.

Now truly,
E-mails run faster,
Emotions run slow.

Everyone Aquarius


The Water-bearer
Says, "I know!"
So do others,
And I,
Ranging between nil
And infinity.

You and I
Have information
And knowledge galore.
It's better to be that way
Than to look inside
Our empty vessels
For wisdom.

9 788819 342300 4